PRETTY, PRETTY PANDA

Nicole R. Harrington

Illustrated by Beatriz Mello

Illustrations by Beatriz Mello
Editing by Janet Brown, Ellaine Kiel, Annie Perez, and Chelsea Tornetto

ISBN: 979-8-89109-505-2 (paperback)
ISBN: 979-8-89109-506-9 (ebook)
ISBN: 979-8-218-28636-1 (hardcover)

First edition 2023

Visit: www.nicolerharrington.com

[Instagram] @bynicolerharrington

[Facebook] https://www.facebook.com/NicoleRHarringtonauthor

To the one and only Son, through whom all truth and love are found.

To my family, especially my amazing children, Kalyn and Ryder, who inspire and bless me beyond measure.

Also to my mom, who prayed and believed with me for this story to come to pass, and provided so much help every step of the way.

To Ben, Brian, and my dad for their willingness to look, listen, and offer their feedback.

To my encouraging, faith-filled friends who are like sisters, especially Sabrina and Dacia.

❤️ 1 Samuel 16:7
❤️ Esther 4:14

There is a panda bear named Pretty who also happens to look pretty. She has a favorite spot where she likes to go to think and dream. It is in a huge, peaceful sunflower field. One afternoon, near the end of summer and the beginning of fall, she went to the field to try to take her mind off of something that happened at school that day. While she was lying amongst all of the bright, golden sunflowers, it lightly sprinkled rain for a moment, tickling her cheeks and eyelashes.

4

On this day, even though she was in her favorite place listening to the sounds of cardinals singing pleasantly to one another, she couldn't stop thinking about what she heard two others whispering about her in class that day.

She was then reminded of other times her feelings had been hurt by things she had heard others say, who did not even know her.

"DON'T PICK PRETTY TO BE ON OUR TEAM. SHE'S PROBABLY NOT GOOD AT SPORTS."

"I doubt Pretty got a good score on the test. She's too pretty to be smart."

"I doubt that Pretty is very nice or funny either."

"Sure, Pretty is pretty, but not as pretty as the most beautiful pandas."

SMART

"

GOD'S PLAN

y

BEAUTIFUL

T

NICE

...

Even though she did not believe the lies said about her, it still hurt her heart to think about them. *"There's more to me than how I look!"* she said to herself. She was starting to feel angry.

Just then, a white, puffy cloud moved in and pushed away all that she was imagining in the sky. The cloud was the shape of a huge sunflower! Pretty loved sunflowers. *Who doesn't love sunflowers?* she thought.

She jumped up quickly. "Yes, that's it!" she yelled out loud. "Instead of being mad about things that don't matter, I'm just going to love others more! I'm going to start giving sunflowers to everyone I can, even to the ones who have hurt my feelings. Maybe then they'll feel loved and want to pass it on."

As she was staring at the huge sunflower cloud, a beautiful bald eagle flew down through the clouds and landed right in front of her.

"Well, hello there," Pretty said.

"Hello, mister skunk. I'm sorry to bother you. While I was flying over the sunflower field, my glasses fell off, and now I can't see where I'm going," Eagle said.

Giggling, she said, "Well, I'm sorry your glasses fell off, but I am actually a panda bear. I'm not a mister, and I hope I don't smell like skunks sometimes do."

"Oh my, I'm sorry for the mistakes, and you smell just fine to me."
They both laughed.

"My name is Pretty, and I'm pleased to meet you. Would you like help finding your glasses?" she asked.

"I would really like that," said Eagle. "I've never met anyone named Pretty before, but it seems like your name suits you."

10

While Eagle and Pretty were chatting, they both noticed a bright rainbow forming over the sunflower field.

Pretty asked the eagle where he thought his glasses had fallen off. "Wow, I think they might have fallen off near the other end of that rainbow!"

They decided to follow the rainbow through the sunflower field in search of Eagle's glasses. Pretty told Eagle her plan to give away sunflowers to others. He said he would like to help her with that.

As they started walking, Eagle asked, "Do you hear someone crying?"

Suddenly, they came upon an elephant. "Hi Elephant, why are you crying?" Pretty asked.

Elephant looked down with tears in her eyes and said, "I-I just quit the school play. I kept forgetting my lines, and the others in the play were laughing at me."

Through sniffles, Elephant said, "I told them that if they weren't such bad actors, I would remember my lines. That's not even true, but it's too late now, so I guess I–I have to quit."

"It's never too late. How many others are in the play?" Pretty asked. "T–Two," Elephant cried.

Eagle helped Pretty collect two sunflowers. "Go back and apologize for blaming them, and give each one a sunflower. Oh, and here's one for you too," Pretty said.

Elephant's face brightened. "I like that idea!" she said. "I'm going to go memorize my lines right now. I can't wait to play my part!"

Eagle and Pretty kept walking towards the rainbow when they came across a giraffe. "What brought you to the sunflower field today?" asked Pretty.

"I saw the rainbow and wanted a closer look to help cheer me up," he said. "Ugh, I don't get to start on the basketball team. Hear me out. The coach said I'm not quite as tall as the other giraffes, and I still need to practice some skills. I was so mad that I tripped the best player as we were leaving practice. I thought it would make me feel better, but I only feel worse."

Eagle picked a sunflower for Giraffe. "Here's a sunflower to take with you to help make you happier," he said.

Giraffe replied, "I don't deserve a sunflower after what I did. I'll take it to give to the player that I tripped, though."

Pretty handed Giraffe another sunflower. "Why don't you keep one and give the other away?" she said.

"Sunflowers *are* pretty cool," said Giraffe. "After I give away the sunflower, I'm going to practice more. I want to be the best teammate I can be!"

Pretty told Eagle that she thought they made a great team.

Eagle agreed and said, "I never thought that losing something could lead to so much happiness! I think we're getting closer to where my glasses might be."

They suddenly felt like someone was watching them. Just then, a fox popped out from between the sunflowers.

Oh, hello, Fox, where did you come from?" Pretty asked.

"What's up, bros! I was just wandering around when I came across this sunflower field. I was like, *Whoah, those sunflowers are lit*, so I came to check it out, ya know? Then I saw you guys, so I have been watching to see what you two dudes were up to."

"So you saw us giving out sunflowers?" Pretty asked. "Would you like to take some with you when you go?"

"Nah," said the fox. "I don't need one, and I don't have anyone to give any to either. I mean, even if I did, giving out flowers would like ruin my reputation, ya know? My favorite thing to do is play video games, but I don't have a lot of friends to play with because they think I'll cheat. It's kind of a bummer, 'cause I slay at gaming, but I wouldn't cheat to win."

Pretty replied, "Maybe you could invite your gaming friends to hang out so you get to know each other better. Sometimes you just have to be a friend to have a friend."

Eagle said, "Yeah, maybe you could come to the sunflower field and play hide-and-seek?"

Fox said, "Maybe someday."

"If not today, then when?" replied Eagle.

Fox then disappeared as quickly as he came, before they could even say goodbye.

Pretty said, "I wonder why Fox did not want to take a sunflower?" I thought everyone would want a sunflower to keep or to give away. Maybe this wasn't such a great idea after all."

Eagle said, "Just offering someone a sunflower makes them feel special and more loved. Elephant and Giraffe are already spreading love to others with sunflowers, and Fox may come back around. Everyone deserves a second chance, and Fox just might take his."

"You're right, Eagle, let's keep going. Look! There's the end of the rainbow!" Pretty exclaimed.

They rushed to the edge of the field, where the rainbow ended. Sitting on the ground below were Eagle's glasses, without a scratch on them. "We did it! We found the glasses!" They both yelled with excitement. Eagle and Pretty hugged and said their goodbyes. "Thanks for your help, Eagle; don't forget to take a sunflower!" Pretty said.

The next day, as Eagle flew back over the sunflower field, he could see many creatures of all kinds walking towards the field from different directions. Fox was walking with his new friend, Raccoon, when he looked up and gave Eagle a nod. Eagle could see they were all coming to collect sunflowers to then go and give them to others, just as Pretty had hoped for. Elephant and Giraffe were coming back to get more too. Eagle smiled, knowing that perhaps Pretty had come to this place for such a time as this.

When Pretty got to her favorite spot that day, she found a note attached to a sunflower. The note read: "Even though I need my glasses to help me see better, more importantly, you helped me to see how to spread more love and happiness to others. You should be called Pretty, Pretty Panda. You are pretty both inside and out!

P.S. Sorry, I thought you were a skunk when we first met. Every time I see a sunflower, I will think of you."

Pretty smiled, looked up at the sky, and saw a heart-shaped cloud above her. She knelt amongst the sunflowers with her arms stretched wide, feeling the warm breeze, thankful for the sunflower field and excited to see what this day would bring.